TABLE OF CONTENTS

Preface

The PhD Process

PhD Failure Rates

The Relationship Between You and Your Advisors (and University)

How To Pick Your Advisors and Your University

Feel Out Your Advisors

How To Stop Your Advisor Trying To Take Advantage of You

    Social Media

    Establish Yourself as a PhD Student

    Representation

    Conferences

    Alarm Bells

Conclusion

PREFACE

So, you're either thinking about doing a PhD, or you made into your PhD program (if it's the latter, then congratulations! That's a big achievement already).

Either way, there are some things you need to know before you start. Some vital pieces of information that you won't find readily. The simple reason for that is because your universities and/or academics don't want you to know.

I'll let you in on a little secret – a fact that isn't too widely published.

Do you know that 85% of people who start their PhDs never finish?

That number goes for national and international rate.

15% pass rate!!! That's horrendous!

That means that 5-in-6 students will not get their PhDs.

The next time you're around 5 of your PhD students buddies, look at them – know that five of you aren't going to make it, only one will. I wonder which five of you won't get PhDs.

That's heartbreaking considering how hard PhD students work, the conditions that they have to put up with, and the sacrifices they have to make.

This book is about how to setup your PhD in the first 12 months to ensure success. To turn those truly horrible stats around.

If you're happy to run the gauntlet alone, then by all means, stop reading. If you're staggered by those numbers (as I am), then you need to read on.

Oh, by the way, I have a PhD from a very reputable University – I got my PhD despite most not wanting me to (I know the ins-and-outs, the things that most people don't, which is why I got my PhD and why most others don't). Also, I have 15 years of experience with the PhD process, from all the different angles, from hopeful applicant, to student, to passing, to having my own students, to developing PhD programs. My knowledge of the PhD process, and how to make sure you pass, has gone up by 8-fold since I finished my PhD, so while I knew how to pass back then (and I used that knowledge successfully), now, I know even more tricks to the system, many political tricks, tricks that most Professors don't even know.

This book is a sister-book to one I wrote earlier entitled "Do you want your PhD now? The PhD Student's Stratagem". That book is geared towards all PhD students, and holds invaluable pieces of information that all students need to pass, but this book is geared specifically to those who are either thinking about doing a PhD, or just starting out in their program (within the first 12 months).

Dr. John Hockey

It details what you need to do in the first 12 months of your PhD to make sure you set yourself up for success.

Let's begin.

THE PHD PROCESS

So, you're thinking about doing a PhD, or just started out. I guess it's a good idea to understand what the PhD process is, what it does (at least, what it's supposed to do), and why it's important.

The PhD process itself is actually quite simple.

It takes someone of a certain level (ability-wise), and trains them to be able to do effective research in a given field. So, you get trained to do two things:

    1) Do effective research.
    2) Do research in a particular field.

That's what the PhD process is fundamentally about! Nothing more, nothing less.

Now, the initial "ability" required by the PhD student is dictated by the University with their entry requirements – there are often prerequisites, like having done a Bachelor's or Master's degree, etc.

Once you're in, the next step is to determine "the question" that your PhD is aimed at answering. This should be done well within

12 months, within 6 months is better. The question is one of the most important parts of the process for the following reasons.

1) The question dictates what you'll be investigating, it doesn't matter what that question is, as long as it is an area of interest. In most cases, this question is geared either directly or indirectly to making money – whether that's investigating how to make a pharmaceutical drug better, or investigating the effects of sleep-deprivation on cognitive functions.

The questions are centered around money because there is funding coming from somewhere. This funding is coming because someone, somewhere, wants to make money out of it. The only possible exception to this is military-funded research, but even then, arguably money is incredibly important – militaries often sell their technology to allies, and they sometimes seek to reduce costs (even they have budgets), etc.

2) Another reason why the question is important is because it needs to be original. There's little point researching something that's been done years ago (unless there's reason to believe that those results will be different now) – doing so would be wasted time, energy, and money. So, the exact question you need to formulate needs to be aimed at investigating something new. For that to happen, you need to be well versed in what's going on in your field. But don't think that you're the only one responsible for this question. In fact, your advisors are far more responsible as they're the experts in the field, you're just the "apprentice". So, it falls on them

to make sure that this question is original and worthwhile.

Once you've formulated your question (remember, your advisors should be taking a very active role in figuring out what the question should be), it's time to plan. The plan needs to be done in detail within the first 12 months. If you don't have a good plan by that stage, then your PhD is and will continue to be erratic (at best).

You need to plan what needs to be done in order to make sure that the question gets answer. It's no good implementing a methodology that won't give you pertinent results. Sure, you can do whatever methodology you want, and you might even get some interesting results, but if they're not pertinent to your question, then there's no way to build a coherent thesis around it – you'll have a little bit from here, a little bit from there, and no comprehensive story can ever be made (funnily enough, some advisors like the "little bit from here, little bit from there" approach, and their students usually pay the price).

Again, making the plan isn't solely up to you – that's what your advisors are there for. (I should stress that, in some countries advisors are called supervisors, but their roles are largely the same – they direct your energy and research so that useful and high quality work gets done. They also heavily influence whether you get your PhD or not, but I'll go into that more later.) Your advisors are experienced in the field, and so they're responsible for making sure of the following:

1) You have a plan.

2) That plan is feasible given the timeframe and resources available.
3) That plan will deliver results that will answer your research question.

The plan ultimately features the methodology, which is the thing that you use to carry out your investigations. The methodology involves processes and equipment (like which equipment to use, how to use it, and how to prepare specimens).

Furthermore, the plan needs to include postprocessing of the data, interpreting the data, finding trends and/or relationships, writing papers, and getting them published. All these items are, again, heavily influenced by your advisors, as they should use their expertise in these areas to make sure that this part of the plan is a success.

These items are also very important for the completion of your PhD because getting all the data but not being able to process it, or draw conclusions, or get them accepted into journals means that that data accounts for nothing! Again, your advisors are very responsible for these items – use them.

Finally, **the plan needs to include the part where you get your PhD** – this is the most important part for you, and unfortunately, it's usually the least important part for the advisors – they get very little out of it. They want research, grant money, promotions, etc. All of those things are either nothing to do with your PhD, or against you getting your PhD – if you leave, then that's research walking out the door (one less person).

So, you can see how straight forward the PhD process is, there's no magic, no mystery, it's very straight forward, and yet, up to 85%

of you will not pass!

That's where this book is designed to kick that number to the curb, and make sure that you're setup for success.

We've already covered the well-known stuff, like "the question" and "planning", etc., but there are more items to cover – items that 99.99% of students don't know about. These items are the ones that determine whether you get your PhD or not.

But before we go on further, let's dig into the statistics a little more and get an idea of how devious they are, and make no mistake, they are very devious.

PHD FAILURE RATES

So, 85% of you won't pass, what a horrendous number. Even 50% is terrible!

But let's unpack that number a little more.

Now, that "won't pass", what does that mean?

That means that 85% of people who **enter** the PhD process will not come out of it with a PhD.

Now, this stat has been heavily massaged by Universities and tertiary education bodies; they say that it includes all those "drop outs" and that the vast majority of people who make it to the defending stage (where you either give your thesis for examination, or give a presentation in front of a grading committee) don't fail – they pass. They go further (to ease everyone's minds) and say that, they won't let a student get to the defending stage unless the advisors and the University (who are usually solely influenced by the advisors' opinions) feel confident that the student will pass.

In other words, they're trying to say that if you make it to the defending stage, then you'll almost certainly pass…**if you make it**.

Now, let's dwell on that "if you make it" for a second, as that "if you make it" is the very thing in your way.

You see, while many people take comfort in that "if you make it", they should actually dread it. That "if you make it" makes you a slave, there's no other way of putting it.

You only get to the defending stage **if** your advisors are happy with your work. That might seem reasonable, as they're the experts, but that's until you realize that they not just experts, they're also people – people who are trying to advance their careers, people who need their jobs for money.

When it comes to gaining things, people are fairly lax when it comes to morality. In fact, most people believe that what's good is what benefits them, and what's evil is what is detrimental to them, so how good will it seem to those people (your advisors) if your passing is detrimental to them? Your passing means that your advisors lose someone who does their research for them, someone who makes them look good. Why would they want you to pass then?? It's detrimental to them.

Some students are not too convinced that advisors are that self-focused, but those people have probably never had a fulltime job, or career. In the real world, people do what they have to in order to get what they want, there's no "niceness" at work – I am yet to have anyone do me any genuine favors, and I've tested this hypothesis out by doing favors for people, and here I am, still waiting for a genuine favor back! You, as the PhD student, are no different, you're just a means to an end for your advisors.

So, that "if" is a thing of beauty. The Universities have effectively devised a way to seem like they're protecting the PhD student, but in reality, all they're really doing is looking out for themselves. Let me unpack that a little more for you:

You're the PhD student, you do research at the University. Universities exist to do cutting edge research, and their academics exist to conduct and direct this research. Without this research, the Universities die. They have their courses, etc., but without the research propelling them to the foreground, their courses mean very little. It's largely the research that dictates how good a University appears. And that appearance is what makes their courses appear good.

PhD students conduct around 65%-75% of the entire research done within Universities – that figure is even higher for some Universities. In other words, you're the lifeblood of the Universities. Without you, the research dries up, and they die. They cannot survive without the research.

So, it's quite easy to see that you're the reason why the Universities are still alive.

If you go, then the amount of research conducted at the Universities will drop, that means less money comes in, which means that the Universities may not survive. The same goes for the academics. If less money comes in, then less positions will be available. Less positions means that someone's head will be on the chopping block (maybe more than one). In addition, less promotions arise, etc. It's bad all round for them.

How well do you think they'll react to that? Do you think that the Universities and academics will just let you go knowing full well (and they're very aware of this fact) that without you, they're futures are uncertain?

The answers to these questions are **NO!!! No, No, No!**

Without you, their survivals are uncertain, but here's the genius part: they control your fate!

If they don't want you to even get to the point where you can defend your thesis, then you won't – the vast majority of Universities require a PhD student's advisors to sign off on their thesis before the defense. **If the advisors don't sign off, then the PhD student doesn't get the chance to defend.** It doesn't matter if the PhD student has been at the University for 10 years, published 20 international journal articles, if the advisors says no, then the student doesn't even get the chance to defend – they can never pass!

But don't fear, they'll just become one of those 85% of people who "didn't pass", not "failed", but just "didn't pass".

Does that sound good?

I hope you're starting to realize the precarious position you're in.

Let me give an idea of how full of shit some advisors and Universities are (excuse the poor language, but there is little way around it – you'll understand when you read the next lines):

I knew this one woman doing her PhD, she wanted to defend – she had done everything necessary, by the book, ticked off all the requirements as per the University's rules, except that her advisors didn't approve. They said that "she'd probably fail." Instead, she should continue her research and wait a little longer. This woman was in an unfortunate position, but far better than most PhD students – her University was actually okay with a student defending against their advisors' wishes (that's far more than 99% of all PhD students get, including myself). So, she decided to boycott her advisors and go ahead with her defense. Do you know what the result was? She passed with flying colors, no corrections, no problems, the best possible outcome. Very few PhD students ever get that grade. And yet, her advisors (in their infinite wisdom) said that she would fail. Why is that I wonder?

The reason is because her advisors were getting research out of her. The longer she stuck around, the more research they'd get. So, it was in **their** best interests to keep her there. While a student getting their PhD is good publicity for the University, they'd far prefer the research. When the student finally gives up, realizing that they'll never be able to defend, they become part of the "85%" who "didn't pass". I know many students who succumbed to this tragedy.

It's not because they're slackers, it's not because they didn't have what it took to get their PhDs, it's not because they didn't have the brains, **it's because they simply weren't allowed to get their PhDs**. There are no good reasons, only that their advisors (and Universities) were greedy. They wanted more research! More, more, more!

Now, the Universities are okay with that stat because of how they present them. By presenting the stat as people who "didn't pass", or those who simply "dropped out", they take all the onus off of the Universities and advisors, and place it on the students – "they didn't have what it takes." At the end of the day, it doesn't matter what it takes to get a PhD, those students were never going to get there simply because the people between them and their PhDs were not going to allow it – I was in that same boat, but as I've said before, I had a few tricks up my sleeve ;).

Let me give you another example: I used to work with another PhD student. This PhD student was decent, not great, but not bad. He did his work well, and had a good head on his shoulders. In order for him to get his PhD, he needed a couple of journal papers – that was a requirement of the University, which is fair enough. Furthermore, he had to be the first author on them in order for them to count.

He had one paper already, and he was doing some more research to get that second paper. He did the research, then wrote the paper. He was quite happy because, he was so close to getting his PhD, and the road was long in getting there. Why was the road long? Well, you'll find out in a second:

He gave the paper to his advisors to review (as you should before submitting it to a journal), and they read it. The problem was that, they did no corrections to the paper, instead, they put their names in front of his and submitted the paper to a journal. In essence, they nullified that paper from being considered part of the 2-paper requirement for him getting his PhD. The University didn't care.

Not long after, he found out – imagine how livid he was. Soon after, he became one of those "85%" of people who "don't pass". Those good for nothing "drop outs!" – excuse my sarcasm.

Who was he to think that he could go on to defend? I mean sure, he'd done everything by the book, he technically had met every requirement (if it weren't for his advisors), but still…that "drop out!"

You know what happened then? His visa expired and he was then shipped back to "whatever country he came from". Thank you for the 5 years of your life, it was fun, we got a lot of research, but now we must go our separate ways...sorry you got nothing out of the deal, sorry that you had to put up with a pitiful wage, sorry that you had to work like a dog, sorry not sorry.

I have many more examples just like that, and I've witnessed them all myself.

You might be wondering how the Universities can still tolerate such a horrendous stat, even if you factor in the effects of their devious words at nullifying much of the negativity of the stat.

A final reason is because having such a high failure rate (and it really is a failure rate, it's not a "didn't pass" rate, because these people were never afforded the opportunity to defend in the first place. They were dragged through the mud. So, in essence, the stat **is** the failure rate, nothing else) makes the degree all the more prestigious.

The harder it is to get, the higher esteemed the degree becomes – that's good publicity for the Universities. So, they manage the negative aspects of the stat (blame the PhD students), while reaping the benefits of that same stat – it truly is an elegant model... horrific, but elegant.

Now, some of you might be thinking, "yes, but how about those students that just weren't smart enough?"

Well, isn't that what the entry exam (or requirements) is for? Isn't that why the University has such a thing?

It's not because they're too stupid, or because they're not motivated, etc. It's because of the system – it's because PhD students are the slaves of the advisors and University. I know because I used to be one.

<u>But</u>, just because you're a slave, doesn't mean that you're powerless. That's where I come in. That's the art of politics – being able to create power from seemingly nothing.

From herein, we get into how to overcome these problems. I give you ways to gain power and set yourself up for success within the first 12 months.

This book is for people just starting out (or thinking about starting out), so I go through several very powerful tactics. I go into them in depth, as you're not as familiar with system as those who've been in their PhDs for a couple of years – and that's alright, we all have to go through the process to learn what the system is – I had to as well.

That book I mentioned earlier ("Do you want your PhD now?") is harder hitting – it's condensed and very powerful. I go through some similar topics in this book as that one, but I tease them out more here. That other book has more topics, and I recommend you to read it, but only after you've gone through this book and understood everything.

Once you've got to grips with this information, then you're ready for the next book, it's hard-hitting, and like this book, it is not very expensive, and trust me, you don't want to pay the price for

Dr. John Hockey

having to find out the hard way (it cost me far more than money to learn the information I present).

Now, we know the well-known items that need to be done within the first 12 months, some stats showing that just doing those items will lead you up s*** creek without a paddle. So, it's obvious that something's missing. Some items that make all the difference between success and failure.

Let's continue with these items! The items that actually matter!

THE RELATIONSHIP BETWEEN YOU AND YOUR ADVISORS (AND UNIVERSITY)

Most of your PhD life will be spent interacting with your advisors and the University.

To that end, it is important to understand what the relationship is among you, your advisors and the University?

The relationship between your advisors and University is quite simple – the advisors do the University's bidding. They're the voice and hands of the University. If the University wants something done a certain way, then it's up to the advisors to carry it out.

The advisors represent the University.

The role between you and your advisors is a little more complicated.

Dr. John Hockey

You're there to do research. This research is good for your advisors (and by extension, the University). You're effectively the apprentice, learning how to do research. After certain criteria are met, then you get your PhD...at least that's theoretically how it works. Often something goes missing between the theoretical part and the practical part (politics is the reason).

An important point to note is that advisors are far more important to the University than PhD students – PhD students get paid far less, many students are advised by one advisor, students don't bring in much money to the University, etc.

As a result, advisors are far more valuable. If you want to know how expendable you are, just look at how valuable you are. An advisor is far less expendable than a PhD student – if something goes wrong, just blame a PhD student. Afterall, "what do PhD students know, they're only "students", advisors are Professors and Doctors, they know what they're doing, PhD students don't know much in comparison", at least that's what people like to think and say.

So, you're expendable and a workhorse. Tough gig. I know the feeling.

Despite walking into this hellhole, how can you get out of it with your PhD?

HOW TO PICK YOUR ADVISORS AND YOUR UNIVERSITY

While many advisors and Universities prey on PhD students, others don't.

To increase your chances of getting a PhD, you need to choose your advisors and University wisely.

Spend time doing so. You're going to spend the next 4 or 5 years there, and it's the place you go to get your PhD (your most important qualification). Choosing poorly greatly determines whether your get your PhD or not (if you end up choosing poorly, then you can still get your PhD – I did – but it will take more work).

Many people, unfortunately, don't have much of a pick of Universities – they often just pick the one in their hometown. That's not the best way, as while it might be financially (or emotionally, if you have family there) easier, **easier doesn't mean better**.

Let me ask you this, which would you prefer:

1) A University with a 20% pass rate?
2) A University 5 states over with a 50% pass rate?

Neither are great, but you are far likelier to pass with the second option, so while it might suck to be away from family and friends, or have less money for the time being, won't it be worth it?

To get an idea of which University to choose, look to their pass rate (the percentage of people who get their PhDs compared to the number of people who **enter** the program).

That single number might be the difference between you getting your PhD and not getting it.

Sure, there are other factors, like the University ranking, or the employment rate afterwards, etc. But does any of that matter if you don't even complete the PhD? I'm guessing (by "guessing", I mean "know") that the employment rate for someone who doesn't complete their PhD isn't quite the same as someone who does.

Similarly, when choosing your advisors, look to their completion rates. You might think that an advisor's completion rate won't reflect yours, and that you'll be the exception. Well, you can think that, but you'd be wrong – I've seen it happen to hundreds of PhD students – there are no exceptions.

If 10% of students finish with one advisor, and 50% with another, then you stand a better chance of finishing with the second advisor.

You might be tempted to think that you should also factor into the equation how reputable the advisor is. That's true, but only if the completion rates among various advisors are comparable – if they're miles apart, then it doesn't matter how much more reputable one is than the other, failing your PhD under a highly reputable advisor still means that you failed. You still get nothing.

Completing your PhD is your first and foremost concern, everything else takes a backseat.

The completion rates of PhD students from Universities are often somewhere on the internet. Sometimes you just need to dig.

The completion rates of an advisor's PhD students are often much harder to find. Most don't advertise such rates (I wonder why). But, it's not impossible.

There's a website called "Google Scholar". Type it in Google and you'll find the link. This website is a search engine for research papers and articles. If you want to find out more information about past students, then this is a good place (if there's nothing on University sites).

What you do is punch in your advisor's name and see what results come up. You'll usually get a list of papers; each paper has the title, a small abstract, number of citations, and the other authors on the paper. That author list is the important part.

Look at which authors were PhD students (it usually says it in the paper). Type these PhD students' names into Google Scholar and see what papers come up for them. See how many there are, when they were submitted for publication (submitting for publication usually means that they were still a PhD student. Some papers are accepted afterwards). This gives you a timeframe of when they were starting to produce results to when they finished producing results. You can add on a year or 1 ½ years to the timeframe (usually it takes a year or so to start getting results and submitting papers). This will give you a good estimate. Try to find these authors' theses, these will often give you dates, like defense dates, or in the acknowledgements, the students will often make references to timeframes (like: "thanks to Joe for being such a great officemate for the last 4 years", etc.).

After finding these past students, look up their names on LinkedIn, ResearchGate, and Google in general. You should get more information about whether they completed their PhDs (they'll have Dr. in their titles), the timeframes (LinkedIn, for example, often has dates). Those students who never published any papers won't show up in your analysis, but that's fine, you'll still get a good idea from considering those who did do at least one paper. Most students get at least one publication out, even if it's a conference paper. In my experience, only about 5% of students who enter the PhD process don't get at least one publication in their time.

Alternatively, if you know people at the University, ask around, but only those whom you trust. You don't want people blabbing to your potential advisors that you're thinking about these things – it might raise some red flags. You don't want to have yourself pegged as a potential "troublemaker" before you start. I'll get more into this later on.

The history of your potential advisors and Universities is the best indication – it doesn't lie. Your potential advisors and Universities can say all they want, but it doesn't mean anything. The history is full of **facts** not just words.

So, once you've picked your advisors and Universities, what's the plan? What do you actually need do in the first 12 months to set yourself up for success?

FEEL OUT YOUR ADVISORS

Within the first 12 months, you need to figure out what your advisors are like. That means that you need to understand their temperaments (are they quick to anger, are the aloof, are they schemers, are they liars, are they honorable, are they fair and just, are they selfish, are they just plain turds, etc.).

One thing that people just can't seem to get their heads around is that, advisors, Professors, Associate Professors, Presidents, etc. are no more moral than anyone else. Just because they've got to those positions doesn't mean that they're good people (in fact, it often means the opposite – they're looking out for themselves). But for some reason, society thinks that these people are model citizens. I, too, used to think like that before I begun my PhD. My eyes were opened wide and quickly.

I quickly found out how immoral (and amoral) many of them are – they're just regular people.

One thing I didn't understand before starting out was that, Academia is essentially just one big pissing contest – who can piss the farthest. Academics love to hear their names mentioned (I know because I'm one too!). Yell the loudest and everyone will think that you're right. I've been in conference presentations where heated arguments have broken out (and by heated, I mean almost fighting). Academics are very egotistical. With that, often comes the inability to see beyond themselves – what they want is really all that matters, everything else is just "in the way".

By understanding what your advisors are like, you can more easily figure out how to act around them and how to plan for success. Let me explain.

If you know that they're having a hard time at work and their job's on the line, then you can bet that they'll be far more willing to take advantage of you. If you see that they're highly ambitious, then expect to be working for them (and I mean it in the sense that, they expect that you should benefit them before anyone else, including yourself).

If they're racist, and you're on the wrong side of the spectrum, then expect some hard times to come. Oh, what's that?...you didn't think that racism would be an issue, and that academics are above it? On the contrary, I've seen it rife in some academic circles. I remember one academic who I worked with (after I had my PhD and was "one of them") say to me that she didn't want anymore people of a certain color in her group (I won't mention which color, as I've seen it work every which way you can imagine, and been on the receiving end of it once or twice), and sure enough, the next two people in her group were not of that color! I haven't heard about her since, so I don't know how that's working out for her.

In addition to understanding their pet-peeves, prejudices, and temperaments, you need to understand how intelligent they are.

How intelligent they are in your field, in academia, and just in general.

If they're slow witted, then you know that you should be able to win in an argument against them (and so your plan can feature accordingly: there may be times in the future where you'll need to argue against them – knowing their strengths and weaknesses when arguing is of paramount importance).

Knowing how intelligent your advisors are in your field is very useful, as you will better understand whether their instructions are worth following (if your advisors are top in the field and they know a lot about your topic, then their ideas on a subject will usually been pretty insightful, unless they're trying to lead you astray. On the other hand, if your advisors don't know much about your field, then following their instructions could be about as useful as rolling dice).

If your advisors are not very knowledgeable in your field, then you need to figure out the plan that your PhD should follow and subtly direct them to it in a fashion where they think that they came up with it (again, if they're slow witted, then you can play to that). I know that devising a PhD plan seems far too much for a new PhD student to do (imagine, someone with little experience in academia having to plan out a 4-year project), but it's doable! I guarantee it!

I've seen it done by many other students, and I did it myself. In fact, I did it myself with my advisors purposefully trying to lead me astray – think about that for a second. I was a young PhD student, with only 6 months under my belt, and I had to plan my entire PhD project while I had people over my shoulder telling me wrong things on purpose. Guess what the result was, I got my PhD and within the allotted timeframe. So, merely planning your PhD is quite easy.

The reason why many people think it's hard is because of the illusion created around the PhD process. As I said earlier, academia likes shrouding PhDs in mystery – it makes them seem more difficult to attain, and people revere them more. In reality, the PhD process in incredibly easy, it's just the politics that makes it difficult.

Anyone with a can-do attitude can plan their PhDs and successfully complete them. Even a greenhorn can. I've seen students in their first 6 months do it successfully. I've also seen students after 3 years of following their advisors' advice achieve about as much as those who are planning on their own do in 1 year (or worse!).

I've had conversations with PhD students, who followed their advisors' advice, as follows:

Me: How long have you been going in your PhD?

Student: About 2 ½ years.

Me: Alright, what's it on?

Student: I don't know.

It's surprising how often that exact conversation comes up.

Another important reason for understanding how intelligent your advisors are in your field, is that you can determine what their motives for having you as a PhD student are. Let me explain.

Your advisors want you as a PhD student for a reason (maybe for more than one reason). They have their own motives, motives that you probably aren't aware of, but you can figure them out. For example, if your advisors don't know much about your field, then you have to ask the question, "why did they want me as a student then?"

What possible benefit could come from it?

Well, it could be because their current field is dead (no more money coming in), and they're looking to branch out into other fields, or that they're looking to expand their horizons so that they look good to their superiors, and thereby increase their chances of promotion.

It could be because they pegged you as someone who is going places, and they want to hitch a ride, or that you'll be useful in a political battle. None of these things work in your favor.

That last point, about political battles, is often lost on students, especially new ones. So, let me elaborate.

What most students don't realize is that, your advisors are employed at the University, it's their jobs, it's their livelihoods. And many of them are ambitious! To get ahead in this world, you have three choices:

    1) Make yourself look better.

2) Make your competition look worse.

3) Wait for the world to change to your benefit.

The third option is about as useful as slapping a couple of fishes together and chanting some magical words – it probably won't work!

The first option is, by far, the more sociably acceptable way, however, two problems arise with adopting only this approach.

The first is that you can only become so good in a given amount of time. The second is that, when people feel threatened, their immediate reaction is to fight back (in this case, to make everyone else look worse). What's more, when people feel threatened, the idea of improving themselves takes a backseat – they feel that they need to deal with this immediate threat now – self-improvement can wait. The problem is that threats are never gone for long – before long, a new threat will always appear. So, while it would be nice if everyone just tried to become as good as they could, in reality, it doesn't often work that way.

Even those advisors who work on their self-development will often succumb to targeting their rivals at work – by eliminating the competition, their ascent to the top becomes easier.

That's where you enter.

By using you as a political pawn, your advisors could make their rivals at work look bad, in which case, they would give themselves the advantage the next time a promotion opportunity comes around.

I don't want to get too much into this, as I detail this particular scenario in my other PhD book ("Do you want your PhD now?") – it goes into great depth. But I do want to give you the heads-up about it as you need to be aware of this from the start of your PhD – while your use as a political pawn typically comes a little later on in your PhD (usually, the longer your PhD drags out, the more useful you are to your advisors in political battles as you're emotionally worn-out, and thereby easier to manipulate), you could face some of these situations within the first 12 months still. I'll get into how to setup yourself up to deter being used as a political pawn, or being used in any way a little later on in the "How To Stop Your Advisors Trying To Take Advantage of You" section.

So, it's obvious now that you need to size up your advisors as soon as possible. The quicker you can do that, the quicker you can devise a plan for your PhD that will stop it getting derailed – you don't want to become that 85%, do you?

The question now remains, how do you size up your advisors?

From the personality side, all you have to do is observe. To ascertain what someone's character is like, just observe how they interact with people who can't do anything for them. The effectiveness of that method may be lost on some, so I'll elaborate:

You see, humans are highly social creatures. Some of the most basic elements about us are aimed at interacting with others. Even our ability to speak is testimony to that. We use these tools, like speech, to manipulate others into getting what we want. Some people might get a little squeamish by the word manipulate, but in the true sense of the word, it is.

Even the very act of saying "please" and "thank you" are designed to manipulate those whom we say them to – we use it as a sign of respect in an effort to make sure that they don't feel the need to attack us.

If you want to see what your advisors' true characters are, just observe how they treat people who can't do anything for them. The reason is because these people have nothing to offer your advisors, and as such, there is little reason for your advisors to "keep up appearances". As such, their true-selves will be on display.

Questions you need to ask yourself are: "do they treat those people fairly?", "Do they treat them with respect?", "Are they quick to anger?", "Are they malicious?", "Are they disrespectful?"

By finding the answers to these questions, you discover their true characters. If their characters are poor, then that doesn't bode well for you. They'll likely try to take advantage of you.

Sizing up your advisors' intellectual side takes a bit more work on your part – you need to get good at your field, but that helps you now and later.

Getting good at your field, knowing what has gone on in your field over the past 15 or 20 years, understanding trends and relationships, and developing "feels" for circumstances in your field (like, being able to predict what would happen if "this" and "that" interacted, etc.) allows you to figure out how much your advisors know about your field.

If you ask them a question and their answer is wrong, then you get a feel for their level of knowledge. Asking more and more questions will give you a better picture. Note that, you should only ask questions as if you want to earnestly learn about the field – remember, you're a new PhD student, you're not supposed to know much about the field, so asking questions in an effort to learn is very acceptable! Going to your advisors with a problem and seeking some clarification is perfectly acceptable. It also gives you an idea of how good they are in your field – if they can't solve the problem, then they might not be very good at the field.

People often asks questions to get an answer, but they rarely use them to test how intelligent someone is. It's a trick you learn as you get older.

Once you've sized up your advisors, then you can determine how to approach your PhD: should you listen to them? Do they know what they're doing? Can I trust their judgement? Do they have my best interest at heart? etc.

HOW TO STOP YOUR ADVISORS TRYING TO TAKE ADVANTAGE OF YOU

For many advisors, it's very tempting to take advantage of their students.

I once heard one advisor say that his PhD students were his army. I swear that I heard one say that. Many think the same way!

But there are ways to heavily discourage your advisors (and University) from trying to take advantage of you.

In your first 12 months, there are 5 things you need to do. (When you progress through the years, there are other things you need to do, but first thing's first! Let's focus on these first 12 months!)

Dr. John Hockey

Social Media

I love Social Media. Not because I like being connected to everyone and seeing what they had for dinner, or the latest update about their knitting, but because of its power.

If you understand how to leverage Social Media, it can become an incredibly powerful tool (weapon) against your advisors. I'll explain how in this section.

About 15 years ago, I came across this idea that over the last 50 years, the world had started to develop a global "social conscience". It came about because the world became far more connected – people on one side of the world could now contact people on the other almost instantaneously. Information could be transferred almost instantaneously. Your friend in Europe could pass judgement on something that happened in Seattle, and vice versa. As such, the entire world was starting to develop a collective conscience.

Over the last 15 years, Social Media has made that interconnectivity explode, and now, it's normal to interact with people from all over the world with one touch of a button.

That's great for sharing information, it's not so great if that information makes you look bad. **That's the power of Social Media.**

You see, your University trades on reputation. People go there because it is seen as reputable.

Reputation covers everything from the quality of the work, to the quantity, to the ethical standards, etc.

As the old saying goes, "The world is getting smaller", and with Social Media, a socially unacceptable act done in the middle of nowhere can be broadcasted all over the world and people in New York, L.A., London, Paris, Shanghai, Tokyo, Rio, etc. all hear about it.

Being able to contact millions of people all around the world within seconds is power!

How does that help you?

It helps you if you know how to leverage it.

How do you think your advisors would feel if they knew anything they said or did could make it out to 20,000 people within 5 seconds?

How do you think they would feel if they knew that anything they said or did to you could make it onto the front page of the newspaper tomorrow morning?

I bet that they'd need some new underwear after realizing that. They'd have beads of sweat pour from their face, their little knees knocking together, and their cup of coffee shaking in their hand.

They don't want to be under the microscope. They don't want every little action scrutinized. Few people can handle being in the public eye.

If you had a Twitter account with 20,000 followers, then that's exactly the type of pressure that you'd be putting on them. If they knew that at will, you could just take out your phone, and send a message to thousands of people detailing their faux-pas, then they'd think twice (thrice, or even ten times) before trying to take advantage of you.

That's the power of Social Media.

Master it, and you will have far more power in your PhD than anyone else.

So, as soon as possible, start Twitter, Facebook, Instagram, LinkedIn, and ResearchGate profiles (and any other Social Media channel). Start getting as many followers as you can! Do it now!

The more followers you get, the more power you'll have. The easiest way to get followers is by following other people. Follow others doing their PhDs, Universities, academics, etc.

Build you follower/friends base, so that if anything ever goes wrong, you've already got a way to mobilize tens of thousands (or even hundreds of thousands) of supporters. Join groups, follow other PhD students as (and for) support.

If every PhD student in the world followed every other PhD student, then that would give every PhD student so much more power – the power to make sure that the PhD process is fair on the PhD students. Don't be stingy on following people or following them back! The more support you give, the more that you'll get in return (you can even follow me on Twitter!).

By building your Social Media contacts, you build your political power. You essentially hold a gun to your advisors' heads (metaphorically, of course) and force them to do the right thing – **some people need more incentive than others to do the right thing**, remember that.

Now, it's important to note that you should not let your advisors or University know that you have this kind of following before you get accepted into your program – if they get wind of it, then they might reject your application – they know the power of these Social Media platforms too.

It's not too hard hide your profile, just use a fake name that you can change at any time after you've become "established" as a PhD student.

Now, onto how to establish yourself as a PhD student.

Dr. John Hockey

Establish Yourself as a PhD Student

At the end of the day, your advisors are established in academia, your University is established. People give their opinions attention because of it. A new PhD student is just a student. Sure, they might be bright, but they're a new student nonetheless.

As such, your opinion doesn't count for much, I'm sorry to be so blunt, but it's true. Let me illustrate my point.

Say you have an argument about some research with your advisor. They say that it's not good enough, but you argue differently. It doesn't matter if you're right, your advisors are more established, and as such, they have the louder voice – remember, the loudest voice wins.

Now, taking that to the extreme, if you get kicked out of your PhD program, your advisors and University can come up with whatever story they want – they could say that you didn't know what you were doing, etc. You, being the student, can't say too much about it, as people automatically place more importance on your advisors' and University's words (because they're established in the field) than yours.

As such, it is your task to become established in your field as quick as possible.

Under normal circumstances, you cannot hope to overthrow your advisors' opinions when it comes to the field, but that's not the purpose.

The purpose is to establish yourself so that you can't be "white-washed":

Imagine that you're a new PhD student, and you have no research under your belt, no one knows you (in the academic world), you have no papers published, how much do you think your opinion is worth?

Relatively speaking, it's not worth much. So, whatever an academic, or your University, says will be taken as true.

Alternatively, imagine that you've got a paper under your belt and some people in the field know you. Now, your advisors' opinions still carry more weight, but yours has some weight behind it now too. If they say that your quality is poor, then you've got evidence to the contrary (papers published, compliments from other researchers, even compliments from your own advisors). You can use that to nullify their arguments.

As such, **within the first 12 months of your PhD, you need to become established**. The more established you become, the more political power you'll have, and as such, it is harder for your advisors and University to treat you unfairly and get away with it.

So, establishing yourself in the academic community and your field is important, and you need to do this within the first 12 months, but how do you do it?

The way to become established is to get your name out there. That means building your social following, going to a conference (and hopefully presenting, but I'll get a little more into that later

Dr. John Hockey

on), becoming well-known among the people at your University, and getting some kind of publication done.

Many people think that getting a publication done in the first 12 months of your PhD is impossible, it's not – I'm living proof.

What's more, if you go to your advisors and express you desire to get a paper (even a journal paper) done within the first 12 months, then your advisors are almost never going to refuse that – they want more papers, they want the notoriety. I can't remember the last time I heard an academic say they didn't want more papers. So, if they do say no to your idea, then you know that something is wrong – that tips you off, maybe they're trying to keep you down – there's a reason for that.

Representation

As a PhD student, you'll have quite a few options for what's called "representation".

"Representation" is effectively someone, or some organization, that will represent you in a dispute – they give you support, whether that's legal or just moral.

Quality representation is always a good idea, but the problem is identifying "quality".

Within the first 12 months of your PhD, you need to identify a representative that is quality and that you can rely on. Then become a member of their group – get their support. Doing this now rather than later is always a good idea – when things go wrong, you want as few things as possible to have to worry about. If you need to deal with the problem (whether that's a dispute with your advisors, a setback in your PhD, or even getting kicked out of the University), you don't want to also have to run around trying to find good representation at the same time. Having to do that means that you can't focus as much on the problem at hand. Also, if you're an established member of whatever group will help represent you, then they will be more willing to help – on the other hand, if a problem arises and you suddenly become a member of a group/organization and immediately ask for help, they will still give it, but they won't be as forthcoming.

Let's go through some of the common options for representation – the good, the bad, and the ugly.

Almost all grad schools have student representatives – you know, where one of your fellow students will have regular meetings with people from the University (HR people, academics, heads of schools, etc.) and bring up issues that the other PhD students have. These student reps also usually help represent you in a dispute.

Relying on them for anything is about as useful as trying to use a brown paper bag as a parachute – you'll come crashing down pretty damn quick! In some cases, the student reps will even become liabilities.

Student reps don't know anything about politics (even if they're political science students, they'll be far outclassed by those they're arguing against – the best way of becoming good at politics is practice, not by having your head in a book – I know that from experience!).

They take those positions largely for the ego-stroke and the extra power they get in their PhDs. But, if push comes to shove, they'll drop you and focus on their own PhDs. Let me get into this a little more.

Student reps are PhD students as well. Their PhDs are far more important to them that you or your PhD. If they start arguing for you, then all an academic has to do is put a bit of pressure on the student rep's PhD and watch the rep fold (remember the brown paper bag – all torn up in a slight gust, let alone plummeting at 100 mph).

Relying on a student rep to help your PhD is a waste of time. But, the rep can be useful if you play them right, you'll be using them, but at the end of the day, that's their job. If they don't want to do their job properly, then they bring it on themselves – I'm not going to get into this political side, as this is usually beyond the 12 month mark.

The other popular type of representation is the Union. Unions are often dubious. There are three types of Unions: ones that get funded directly from the University, ones that get funded indirectly from the University (like through the government), and ones that are purely independent.

The ones that get funded directly from the University are wastes of time. They're not going to undermine the University too much as then their funding will get cut. Most people want to help, but they don't want to jeopardize their own wellbeing in the process. In essence, these types of Unions are for show, they don't do much for the people who they are supposed to represent. Speaking from experience, unionists in these unions often work against you behind the scenes – they often pose as people you can go to and talk with about problems, but they feed that information directly back to the University. So, any idea of how to make your advisors and/or University capitulate will get fed straight back to them, and they'll be prepared when you try to implement your plan – these unionists are scum – they pretend to be on your side, but betray you at the drop of a hat. DO NOT TRUST THEM!

They can be useful though, feed them the wrong information to relay back to the academics and the University, thereby blindsiding them later on. Make them waste their time and energy coming up with plans to foil your "plans", then use a different plan to catch them off guard. I digress though, this is beyond the 12 months mark.

The Unions that get funded indirectly by the University are better, but marginally. At the end of the day, if they cause the University too much trouble, then the University can put pressure on the funding body (even if it's the government, as Universities are often billion dollar organizations, and the government doesn't want to jeopardize that – it'd be bad for the economy) to reduce the amount of funding. So, while these types of unions can do a little more to help, they're still very much on a leash.

The final type of Union, the ones that aren't funded in any way by the University, are often much better. The fees will be higher, <u>but</u> in return, you'll get better representation. The main problem is that these kinds of Unions are few and far between. Most Unions have ties in some way to the University (money-speaking), and so the health of the Union depends on how well they treat the University. What's more, there are two factors that compromise the integrity of these Unions. The first is that some of the members, or even all, probably went to that same University, so they have some political ties there. The second is that if the University ceases to exist, then the Union will cease to exist – if there is no University, then there is no need for a Union. The unionists know this. So again, there'll likely be a temperance to their "gung-ho-ness".

Your job in the first 12 months is to find representation that will genuinely represent you, whole-heartedly, and not hang you out to dry when the going gets tough.

You can do that by looking to the past of any organization claiming to represent the students. See if they hung anyone out to dry in their past. If so, why.

Look at who's in charge, what ties they have to the University, where they went to University, etc.

Try to find anything showing lackluster and nongenuine performance.

Finding good representation will help you immensely in the future. If you cannot find quality representation, then you'll need to take on any argument in the future by yourself. It's not impossible to win as an individual against the many (I won), but it means that you'll have to work harder when the time comes. The upshot of that is that you become far better at dealing with problems, negotiations, and confrontations. Those skills serve you well later on in life – I've reaped countless rewards because of the skills I learnt during that period in my PhD.

Quality representation is not a necessity, but it definitely helps! It makes your life easier, and anything that makes your life easier should be sought after.

A final word about not being able to find quality representation: If you cannot, then you can manipulate the situation to your advantage. When conflict arises, many Universities require the PhD student to have representation. By aligning yourself with the weakest representation body, they'll get called in. All you have to do is break them, then toss them aside. Again, that is later down the track, but you need to prepare for it from the start.

Taking this avenue is useful in that the academics and University won't see it coming. You see, the academics and University have a Standard Operating Procedure (SOP) when dealing with problems and conflicts, especially when it comes to PhD students. Having representation is usually in that SOP. So, they know how everything will play out even before any meetings have begun, they've done it a thousand times before. They know what strings to pull and when. That greatly works against you. It puts you at a major disadvantage. By throwing a wrench in the works, like breaking the representative down, you change the game. You make the situation different, something that they're not familiar with, something that they don't have a plan for. That works to your advantage. Put them on unfamiliar ground, make them improvise, that will draw errors. (But enough about that, that will be far in the future, and this book is just about the first 12 months.)

Conferences

Within the first 12 months, you should try to go to one conference – even better if you present at one!

The reason is because you want to establish yourself.

By going to a conference, you gain national or even international notoriety. You become a face in the field. You don't want to lurk in the shadows, being a PhD student that no one has ever heard of before – that doesn't give you power.

By the second year of my PhD, I had gained an international reputation of being able to make Professors look like fools. Whenever someone got up to give a presentation, they knew that if I wanted to, I could make them look very foolish, very easily.

What benefit was that to me?

It meant that my word was strong – sure I was still a PhD student, and my University would still side with my advisors over me any day of the week. <u>But</u>, internationally, everyone knew that I was far smarter, far better, and if I was kicked out of my PhD due to "a poor quality of work", everyone would've known that it was bulls***. So, that reduced the amount of options my University had. They knew that they couldn't wheel out that story, so their biggest advantage (being intellectually superior to me) was gone on the national and international stages.

You need to do the same thing.

You might be wondering, "but how can I be better in a field that someone who's been doing it for 40 years?"

Simple, learn everything you can about the field. Believe it or not, but science isn't hard – it's just logical. That's the failing of 99% of scientists out there – they might learn a phenomenon, but they never dig down into the basics, and figure out how it's occurring on a fundamental level – they're too focused on "overall" effect. Work on your fundamentals, and everything else will fall into place. Believe it or not, but many Professors have poor fundamental knowledge of their field – that makes them sitting ducks, just waiting for someone to come along and blow them out of the water.

In addition, going through a problem, listing all that you know, and then thinking about all the possibilities for a given phenomenon, then thinking about their likelihoods is incredibly powerful – by doing this, you expose weaknesses, you understand strengths, you understand how likely certain explanations are. What most people don't realize is that science is all about just being methodical – list what you know, what you don't know, and think about why you don't know those things, and how to find out those things.

There's not much more to science than that.

As with most things, it's all in the preparation. By being prepared, you can make almost anyone look like a fool.

A final point on conferences: I mentioned the possibility of presenting at one within your first 12 months. Some students might not believe that it's possible to have a conference paper within the first 12 months of your PhD. Well, it is possible.

To give you an idea of how easy it is to write a conference paper, I once conducted my research, analyzed the data, wrote a conference paper, and submitted it within 3 days. 3 days!!! That conference paper is still getting quite a lot of citations – it was also head-and-shoulders above the other papers presented back then (I was only 18 months into my PhD at the time). The thing that helped me do all those things in only 3 days was inspiration – a great idea hit me and I ran with it. I kind of bypassed my advisors' opinions about whether it was worth pursuing or not by just briefly discussing the idea with them (like I was just spitballing ideas around – if you talk enough, then many people will just start agreeing with you to get you to shut up and leave them alone), then when they expressed a general positiveness towards the idea (to shut me up), I took it as enough to justify conducting the research and writing the paper – my plan was that, if they said that I shouldn't have done it sometime down the track (which they actually did), I could always express how I took their generally positive words about the idea as consent (which is what I argued when this debate came around). As a result, the paper got done in very little time, and my advisors were moved out of my way – all with careful "massaging" of their words and emotions.

Dr. John Hockey

Alarm Bells

Within your first 12 months, you don't want to raise any alarm bells. You don't want your advisors and/or University to realize that you're not going to be a slave like the other PhD students. You don't want them to realize that you're not going to let them treat you unfairly. You don't want give them a reason to kick you out, or make your life difficult while you're still in the "infancy" stage of your PhD.

Many PhD programs have certain timeframes, which within, a PhD can be stopped, and the student can be kicked out, with little reason. It could be due to "funding" or because you "failed" a presentation or exam, etc. Within these timeframes, you don't really get much of a say – the University is omnipotent in this stage. Which is why you should avoid raising alarm bells within this period.

If you raise alarm bells before this stage, then you'll be in a weak position. If you have Social Media power (a strong presence on it), then you can flex some of those muscles, but it still isn't ideal to do so, so early on.

Find out what the timeframe is where they can stop your PhD at will (often it's 6 – 12 months), and don't raise alarm bells before that.

CONCLUSION

So, you made it to the end of the book without getting scared off by what awaits you. Congratulations!

Let's go through some of the key takeaways, and what you need to do within the first 12 months of your PhD to set yourself up for success.

-A PhD is about taking someone of a certain ability and training them to do effective research, in a given field.

-85% of PhD students don't pass their PhDs – most of them get held down until they quit.

-Advisors and Universities are the causes of this horrendous stat.

-Your advisors represent the University, they do its bidding.

-Your advisors stand in between you and your PhD. Without their consent, you don't even get the chance to defend your thesis, let alone pass.

-You need to spend time and energy picking your advisors and University carefully. Pick ones that have good track records. Not track records that show getting a lot of money, or citations, or PhD students, **BUT** track records that show **good completion rates** and short completion timeframes! Do this BEFORE you start!

-Within your first 12 months, feel out what your advisors are like. Figure out whether they'll treat you like a slave, or whether they'll treat you fairly. Whether they're intelligent in your field, or not. Whether they're quick-witted, or not. Whether their PhD students typically finish, or not. How long for PhD completion, etc. All of this will help you figure out how to approach your PhD, whether your advisors will pose a problem in getting your PhD, how to get over them, etc.

-No matter how good your advisors are, they could always become draconian towards you. It could be something personal that develops (academics are just like other people, they're no more mature – in fact in some ways, they're far less mature), or pressures from the University could cause them to become harder on you, and their other PhD students, etc.

-To stop your advisors (and University) taking advantage of you, you need to do the follow within the first 12 months of your PhD:

>-Build a very strong Social Media presence – get as many follower and friends as possible. That gives you a very strong social power.

>-Establish yourself as a PhD student, and as a researcher in your field. Try to get as many people as possible to know about you. That gives you power.

-Find quality representation – figure out which of your options of representation (e.g. union) are high quality and genuine, and which are not (e.g. student reps). Join whichever group offers such a service – it will be very, very useful later on. Sort this out early on, and reap the benefits later, instead of having to rush around to find someone good when you need it.

-Attend (and present at) a conference, meet and greet, and make yourself known as a player in your field.

-Don't raise any alarm bells while your University can kick you out without much of a reason – most PhD programs have a certain timeframe for this to happen (6 month, 1 year, etc.).

That's what you need to do in the first 12 months of your PhD to succeed.

After those 12 months, more factors come into the equation, and they are very manageable, as long as you know how to approach them.

OTHER BOOKS BY THE AUTHOR:

Do you want your PhD now?: The PhD Student's Stratagem

Why most books on "how to get a PhD" are full of S*!**

If you liked this book, then please give it a review. It helps me out, as well as your fellow PhD students – they can recognize a useful resource – this helps you as well, as there'll be more people pushing the advisors and University for better conditions.

Made in United States
Troutdale, OR
01/05/2024

16704640R00040